Little Mitchie

BEING A GOOD LISTENER

MAKING NEW FRIENDS

ANNE ACCARDI

CREATING YOUNG NONFICTION READERS

Little Mitchie books spark curiosity and support early nonfiction reading for students in Grades 2-3. Designed to build vocabulary, support second language learners, and prepare readers for middle-grade content, each book includes helpful tips for parents and educators to build confidence and deepen understanding of the world.

TIPS FOR READING NONFICTION WITH BEGINNING READERS

Talk about Nonfiction

Begin by explaining that nonfiction books give us information that is true. The book will be organized around a specific topic or idea, and we may learn new facts through reading.

Look at the Parts

Most nonfiction books have helpful features. Our *Little Mitchie* titles include color photographs and graphic aids, a table of contents, a glossary, and an index. Share the purpose of these features with your reader.

Color Photos and Graphic Aids

A lot of information can be found by "reading" photos, charts, maps, and other graphic aids found within nonfiction texts. Help your reader learn more about the different ways information can be displayed.

Table of Contents

Located at the front of the book, this list shows the big ideas within the text and the page numbers where they can be found.

Glossary

Located at the back of the book, the glossary defines key words and phrases that are related to the topic. These words and phrases can be found in the text in colored type.

Index

Located at the back of the book, an index is an alphabetical list of topics and the page numbers where they can be found.

With a little help and guidance about reading nonfiction, you can feel good about introducing a young reader to the world of *Little Mitchie* nonfiction books.

Little Mitchie is an imprint of:

Mitchell Lane
PUBLISHERS

2001 SW 31st Avenue
Hallandale, FL 33009
mitchelllanepub.com

First Edition, 2027.

Author: Anne Accardi
Designer: Kathy Walsh
Editor: Kim Thompson

Library of Congress Cataloging-in-Publication Data
Title: Being a Good Listener / by Anne Accardi

Description: Hallandale, FL :
Mitchell Lane Publishers, [2027]

Identifiers:
ISBN 979-8-89260-896-1 (library bound)
ISBN 979-8-90145-053-6 (paperback)
ISBN 979-8-90145-000-0 (eBook)

Library of Congress Control Number: 2026930155

Photo credits: Shutterstock: Cover, p 1 and backgrounds Mangostar; p 5, PeopleImages; p 7 & 14, BearFotos; p 9 & 13, Roman Samborskyi; p 11, fizkes; p 17, Pixel-Shot; p 18, Westock Productions; p 19, Evgeny Atamanenko; p 21, Lopolo

TABLE OF CONTENTS

Step One

KNOW WHY LISTENING IS IMPORTANT

It is fun to make new friends!

Friends play together. They care about each other. They listen to each other.

To make new friends, it is important to be a good listener. Listening shows **respect**. It lets people know you care about their thoughts and feelings. It lets them know you would make a good friend!

"Part of doing something is listening."
—Madeleine L'Engle

Step Two

FACE YOUR FEARS

Making new friends can be scary! It is hard to talk to someone you don't know. Take a deep breath. Remind yourself that they may be just as scared as you are.

If you listen to someone, you will learn more about them. They will get to know you too. This will make you both feel more comfortable.

CHALLENGE

When you feel **nervous**, try this exercise. Take a deep breath in. Hold it for three seconds. Then, breathe out slowly. Repeat until you feel calm.

Sometimes, it is hard to be **patient**. You may be excited to share your own ideas. You might be afraid you will forget what you want to say. That's okay! Stay calm and keep listening. Remind yourself that you'll get your turn to talk.

CHALLENGE

Ask a friend or family member to help you practice being a good listener. Listen carefully as they tell you a story about their day. See how patient you can be.

Step Three

TAKE ACTION!

Are you ready to make a new friend? Be brave. Start up a conversation. Begin by saying, "Hi!" Introduce yourself.

FRIENDLY FACT

Your **body language** can show that you are friendly. Don't cross your arms or fidget. Look at the person. Smile!

Ask your new friend questions. Listen carefully to their answers. Are any of your answers the same? If so, you have something in common!

Here are questions to ask a new friend.

- *What activities do you like to do?*
- *Do you have brothers or sisters?*
- *Do you have a pet?*
- *What's your favorite food?*
- *What games do you like to play?*
- *What do you want to be when you grow up?*

As your new friend answers your questions, be an active listener. That means giving them your full **attention**. Look at them. Do not **interrupt**. Let them finish speaking before you take your turn.

FRIENDLY FACT

Avoid **passive** listening. A assive listener isn't focused on the person speaking. They are thinking about other things.

As your new friend talks, give positive **feedback**. That means showing that you understand and care.

Nod your head. Say things like "uh-huh." Ask follow-up questions.

FRIENDLY FACT

Sometimes, talking is part of listening. Try using your own words to **restate** what your friend said. That shows you listened and understood.

Step Four

KEEP GOING

Once you've listened to someone and found things in common, you have a new friend. Keep getting to know them better. Let them get to know you too.

Then, bring others into your group. Take turns asking questions and listening to each other. You will soon have many new friends!

TOP TIPS

Listen before you talk.

Ask questions.

Find what you have in common.

Restate in your own words.

Make eye contact.

GLOSSARY

attention (uh-TEN-shuhn) focus; concentration on one thing

body language (BAH-dee LANG-gwij) the thoughts and feelings your face and body communicate without using words

feedback (FEED-bak) reactions; information about what others are thinking

interrupt (in-tuh-RUHPT) to start talking while someone else is talking

nervous (NUR-vuhs) worried, scared, or anxious

passive (PAS-iv) unresponsive; not interested

patient (PAY-shuhnt) calm and able to wait

respect (ri-SPEKT) a feeling of admiration and appreciation for other people

restate (ree-STATE) to repeat in different words; to summarize

FURTHER READING

Sauer, Tammi. *Wordy Birdy.* Doubleday Books, 2018.

Stein, David Ezra. *Interrupting Chicken: Cookies for Breakfast.* Candlewick Press, 2023.

Verde, Susan. *Are You Listening?* Harry N. Abrams, 2024.

ON THE INTERNET

RocketKids: Three Ways to Be a Better Listener
youtube.com/watch?v=mnUp7WgZ2TU
Watch a video with three tips for great listening.

Sesame Street: How to Be a Good Friend
youtube.com/watch?v=4ai7ckER2os
Watch this episode about how friends practice kindness and sharing.

INDEX